This book belongs to

For Geoff Lennard (Daddy)—K. L.
For Katharina—E. G.

First edition for the United States, its possessions, the Philippines,
and Canada published in 2009 by Barron's Educational Series, Inc.

First published in 2009 in Great Britain, under the title *Little Genius: Eyes*,
by Red Fox, and imprint of Random House Children's Books
A Random House Group Company

All inquiries should be addressed to:
Barron's Educational Series, Inc.
250 Wireless Boulevard
Hauppauge, New York 11788
www.barronseduc.com

Library of Congress Catalog Card No. 2008931692

ISBN-13: 978-0-7641-4131-7
ISBN-10: 0-7641-4131-7

Printed in China
9 8 7 6 5 4 3 2 1

Hello!

I'm **Young Genius**.

I've been looking into the human body and all the interesting parts that make it work.

This book is about the amazing things on your face called your

eyes.

I'm here to tell you all about them . . .

Did you know that your eyes are actually shaped like balls?
That's why they are called **eyeballs**.

Eyes are in the front of the head because it's a good place to look out from. Anywhere else wouldn't get such a great view!

This is what your head bone (skull) looks like without skin or hair.

Eyeballs sit in the holes (sockets) here.

Can you feel the bones around your eyes?

If you could touch an eyeball it would feel squishy, like a grape!

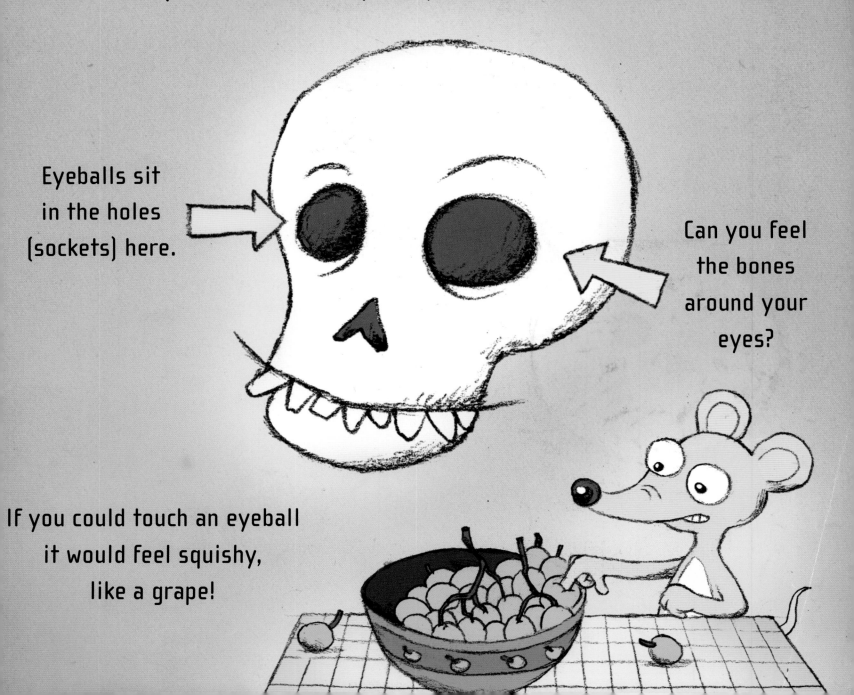

Some animals have eyes on the sides of their head. Good for seeing if anything's coming to get them!

WHACK!

Flies have got hundreds of tiny eyes. That's why they're **really** hard to swat!

A fish's eyes are big and round for seeing in water. Look in here for a fish-eye view!

Let's have a really good look at an **eye**.

The colored part is called the **iris**. You can get blue, brown, green, or a mixture. What color eyes do you have?

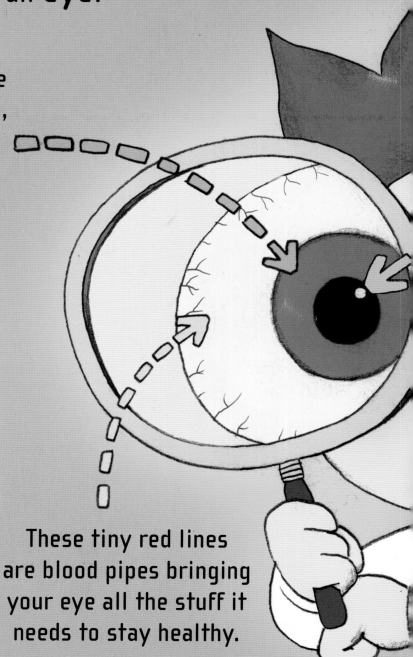

Computers can tell who someone is just by looking at their iris!

These tiny red lines are blood pipes bringing your eye all the stuff it needs to stay healthy.

If you look **really** closely, you can see amazing patterns in the colors of the iris. Everybody has a different pattern!

Your eyes move around wherever you look.

Are you Looking at me?

The black dot in the middle is actually a hole! It's called a **pupil**. A pupil can change size depending on the light.

This is what you'd see
if you cut an eye in half.
This is just a model—
don't ever try it in real life!

This isn't just an empty
space. It's full of clear **goo**
to keep the eye healthy
and squishy.

This part is called
the **lens**. It's like
a see-through
stretchy plate.

The orange
line is called
the **retina**.

Can you see the clear
bump over this bit?
It's called the **cornea**.

goo

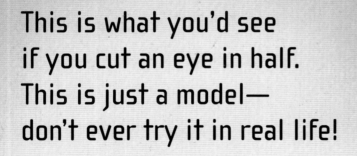

The white is only on the outside, like an orange peel.

There are lenses in lots of other things, too.

telescope

SAY CHEESE!

microscope

magnifying glass

camera

cone

rod

Your retina is covered with tiny sticks. Some are called **cones**. They're for seeing colors.

Some are called **rods**. They're for seeing black and white.

So, how do **eyes** work?

Eyes are like your body's windows. If you don't have them, you can't see out!

When I pull up this blind I'm letting in the light.

That's exactly what your eyes do when they open.
They let in the light!

Everything you see starts off as **light.**

Have you ever looked behind you in a movie theater?

The light shines out from the back, over the

rows of seats, and lands at the front

as pictures on the screen.

The back of your eye is like a movie screen!

The picture goes in upside down!

retina

pupil

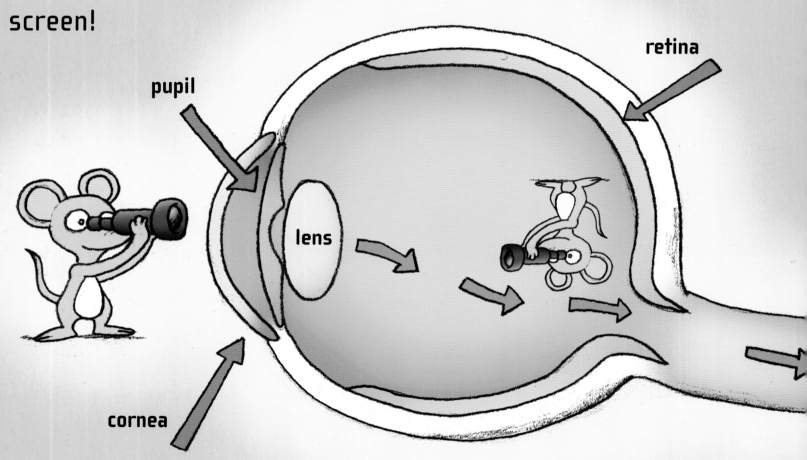

lens

cornea

The picture hits the cornea and is flung down the pupil to the lens, through the goo and onto the retina.

The messages get sent up these wires (the optic nerve) at the back to a big computer called your brain.

Your brain flips it over for you when it gets there. If it didn't, we'd think everything was on the ceiling!

Your **brain** can understand the messages and tells you what you are seeing.

Cats' eyes are bigger than ours. They have larger pupils which let more light into their eyes.

Have you ever noticed the lights in the road at night? They're called "cat's eyes" because the man who invented them copied how a cat's eye works.

He got the idea when a real cat's eyes stopped him from driving into a wall!

Like a mirror, eyes don't work properly if they're dirty.

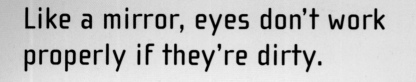

Eyelids are a bit like windshield wipers on a car!

Every time you blink, your **eyelids** come down and give your eyes a wipe.

Eyelashes and **eyebrows** help to keep out dust, too.

Eyes have got a great cleaning mixture called tears. They are made of salty water.

If your eye really hurts or you're upset about something, tears can overflow. They flow down your cheeks and in your nose pipes.

That's why you get a runny nose!

Sleeping is really good for your eyes. It gives them a good wash and a soak.

To keep your eyes healthy and safe, don't:

Read in the dark.

Look straight at the sun.

Use other people's eye drops.

Wear other people's glasses.

Some people have trouble seeing clearly.

An eye doctor will do an **eye test** to find out
if you need glasses.

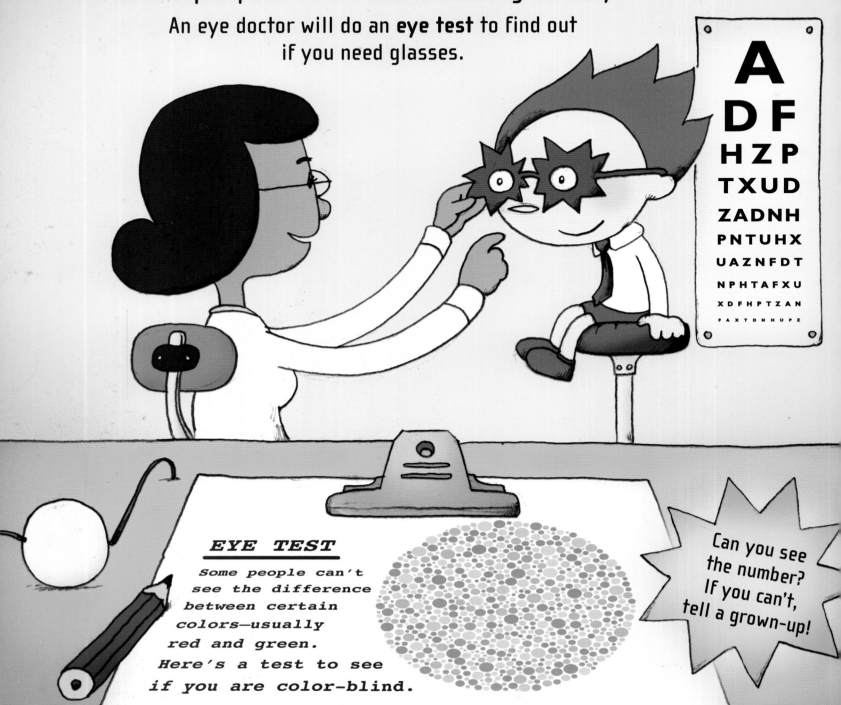

A
D F
H Z P
T X U D
Z A D N H
P N T U H X
U A Z N F D T
N P H T A F X U
X D F H P T Z A N
F A X T D N H U P Z

EYE TEST

Some people can't
see the difference
between certain
colors—usually
red and green.
Here's a test to see
if you are color-blind.

Can you see
the number?
If you can't,
tell a grown-up!

Glasses are fun to choose!

They have lenses to correct any fuzziness.

Some people are blind. This means their eyes don't work. They can have special dogs, called Seeing Eye dogs, to help them get around.

CooL!

ometimes children have condition called "lazy eye." hey have to wear an eye patch ver the good eye so the lazy ye can get stronger and catch up.

Healthy eyes can do great tricks!
Like these:

Is this a duck or a rabbit?

Look at all the dots, are they black or white?

Is this book open or closed?

Stare at this fish and count to 30 slowly.

Now look at the fish bowl. Can you see it go in? What color is it?

That's everything I found out about eyes.

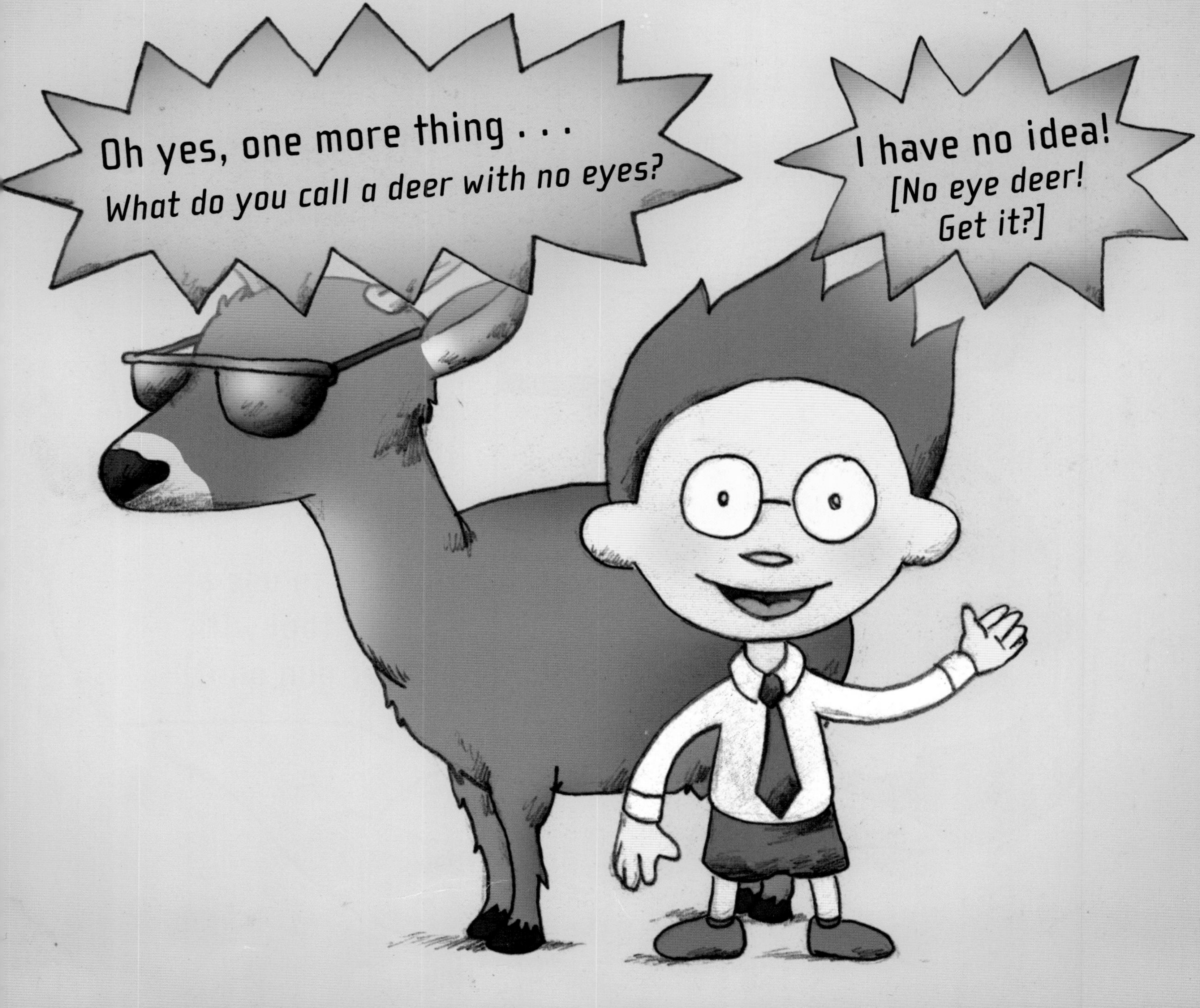

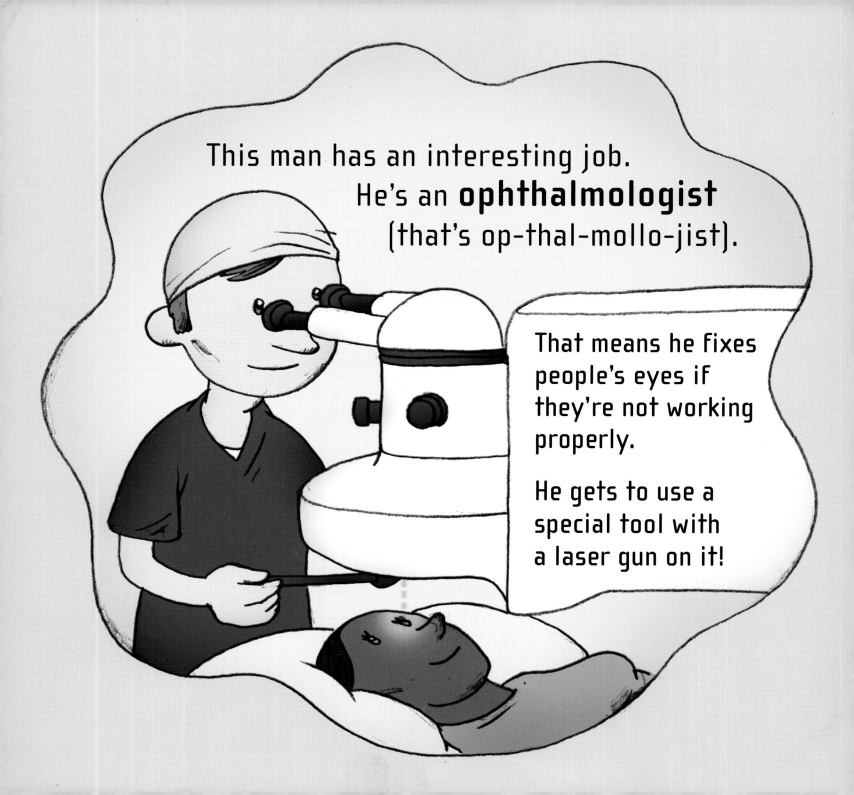

I'd really like to be an ophthalmologist when I grow up.

How about you?

More **Young Genius** books
for you to enjoy

978-0-7641-4130-9

978-0-7641-3670-2

978-0-7641-3669-6

978-0-7641-4131-7